An EYE OPENER for
SMALL MEDIUM
ENTERPRISES
(S M E 's)

An EYE OPENER for SMALL MEDIUM ENTERPRISES (S M E 's)

Mathews Mutale

To order additional copies of this book, contact:
Xlibris Corporation
1-888-795-4274
www.Xlibris.com
Orders@Xlibris.com
128742

CONTENTS

DEDICATION

I dedicate this book to my children:
Kafula, Chileshe, and Nadiela.
Also to my Mother: Ellena Mwansa Mulenga

FOREWORD

Mathews is a great leader and his work with the Diamondale Foundation is a huge credit to himself and all involved with it. He has used his great experience and knowledge in the field of business development to create this book and to offer his advice and tips for anyone currently in the small or medium sized businesses or for someone starting anew.

The book, once picked up can never be put time as you remain gripped to learn the next lesson from Mathews and start to apply your new found knowledge into your own business. I have not yet come across a book like this before and it is both beneficial for the business and project management community; it works by layering each key piece of information so that you can grow and develop as each chapter unfolds.

Mathews uses his simplistic approach and language effectively. His wonderful appreciation of this subject shows his great originality, creativity and credibility to all his readers. I highly recommend this book to anyone already in small business already or someone seeking a new and exciting career by starting up a business of your own in the future.

Mark Reeson FAPM FAAPM PMP GPM

Author of Project Management can Save the World, The P5 Concept – a new vision for Sustainability in Project Management and Project Management for Future Generations

PREFACE

My motivation for writing this text was to provide Small Business Enterprises (SME's) with holistic, integrative view of Marketing and Business Project Management. A holistic view focuses on how Marketing and Business Project Management contribute to strategic goals of an organization. The linkages for integration include the process selecting Marketing strategies and projects that best support the strategy of a particular organization and that in turn can be supported by the technical and managerial processes made available by the organization to bring projects to completion. In the face of intense, worldwide competition many organizations have reorganized around a philosophy of innovation, renewal, and organizational learning to survive. This philosophy suggests an organization that is flexible and project driven.

AUDIENCE

This text is written for a wide audience. I t covers concepts and skills that are used by managers to propose, plan, secure resources, budget, and leads to Marketing/project teams to successful completion of there projects. The text should prove useful to SME's. Our emphasis is not only on how management process works, but more importantly, on why it works. The concepts, principles, and techniques are universally applicable. The text does not specialize by industrial type. Instead the text is written for the individual who will be required to manage a variety of projects in different organizational settings.

NOTE TO SMALL BUSINESS ENTERPRISES

You will find the content of this text highly practical, relevant and current. The concepts discussed are relatively simple and intuitive. As you read, we suggest you try to grasp not how things work, but why things work. You can use this text as move through three levels of competence:—I know, I can do, I can adapt to new situations. Marketing/Project Management involves understanding the cause-effect relationships and interactions among the sociotechnical dimensions of projects. Improved competency in the dimensions will greatly enhance your competitive edge as a Marketer/ Project Manager.

Good luck on your journey through the text and on your future career.

INTRODUCTION

There is no doubt that most African countries depend on their Micro, Small and Medium Enterprise (SMEs) in driving their economies forward. However, most of these SMEs receive lukewarm support from their governments. Nevertheless, a few Competitive SMEs are thriving and contributing to economic growth, employment Creation and local development in combating poverty

SIGNIFICANCE OF SME'S IN ZAMBIA

SMEs are the engine of every nation's economy as they occupy a prominent Position in the development of many countries in the world be it least developed, Developing and developed countries. Contributions of SMEs can be well noted in a Number of aspects including labor absorption, creation of entrepreneurial spirit and Innovation, promotion of linkages and complementary role to large companies, wealth Creation, among others.

STATUS OF SMES IN ZAMBIA

SMEs require special attention for them to Graduate to larger firms. Most SMEs in Zambia have been at a micro level since Inception some decade years ago. This stagnation is not only caused by the lack of Effective public policy to support SMEs but also the entrepreneur's characteristics such as poor education backgrounds

CONSTRAINTS FACED BY ZAMBIAN SME'S

Difficulties in filling capacity Gaps for SMEs

ƒ Poor work culture in public offices, organizations, households and in individual personal lives;

ƒ An attitude of dependency: always expecting government/donor to come up with packages;

ƒ Apathy, believing that we are poor, failing to see potentials that are waiting to be tapped;

ƒ Lack of commitment to desired mission (putting short sighted self interest first and;

ƒ Corruption

SMES' HURDLES IN ACCESSING FUNDS

THE problem of limited access to affordable finance has been a vexing issue for Small and Medium Entrepreneurs (SMEs) in Zambia for many years.

Traditionally, SMEs have problems in accessing financial support because of many factors.

The limitation has been largely as a result of structural difficulties affecting the entrepreneurs more than the lack of windows of financing. These structural limitations have resulted from problems related to lack of financial support, inadequate collateral, inaccurate costing and pricing. All this work to slow down the growth of the entrepreneurs.

CONCLUSION

Empirical studies have shown that the manufacturing sector in Zambia of which more than 80% consists SMEs, is stagnant. The issue at hand for Zambia is to come up with a mix of policies and strategies for unlocking this very important sector so that it performs at the frontier and in return contributes to poverty reduction and economic growth. But the question lies in finding the right "key" to be used in unlocking the SME sector

MARKET PENETRATION STRATEGIES INTO ZAMBIAN

- This involves Teaming and Partnering for Small Businesses (SME's). This covers :-
- Business Capacity
- Types of Teaming Arrangements
- Teaming Agreements
- Mentor
- Teaming Opportunities

BUSINESS CAPACITY

- Most businesses are limited in their ability to qualify for big business. They lack capacity and that calls for Partnering with other entities that can provide them with opportunities to increase capacity.
- The increases in resources allow them to compete for big businesses but some small organizations are not interested because they don't want to share the pies. They don't realize that partnering allows them to go bigger pie.

TYPES OF TEAMING AGREEMENTS

- Prime Contractors and Subcontractors
- Traditional and Non-Traditional
- Subcontracting
- Partnerships
- Limited/ Limited Partnerships
- Joint Ventures

TEAMING ARRANGEMENTS

A significant way to increase business opportunities for Small Business is through teaming arrangements and subcontracting relationships. Teaming arrangements are desirable from a federal and industry stand point because they enable small businesses involved to compliment each other's unique capabilities and offer the government the best combination of performance, costs and delivery for the product being acquired. Teaming agreements may include large businesses and small businesses. There may be size issues involved when small businesses enter teaming agreements. The parties can be considered affiliated and the combined receipts/employees of the teaming partners will determine whether the entity meets the size standard(13CFR 121.103.) NEDA Business Consultants, Inc. can assist you in structuring the teaming arrangements.

WHAT IS
TEAMING ARRANGEMENT?

The Federal Acquisition Regulation (FAR) Subpart 9.6, Contractor team arrangements, describes contractor team arrangements as follows:

"Two or more companies form a partnership or joint venture to act as a potential prime contractor";

or

"A potential prime contractor agrees with one or more other companies to have the act as its subcontractors and a specified government contract or acquisition program";

WHAT IS A MAJOR DIFFERENCE BETWEEN A PARTNERSHIP AND A JOINT VENTURE

- A partnership is a voluntary association of two or more individuals to carry on a business for profit, usually on permanent basis. A limited partnership provides for limited of one or more of the partners.
- A joint venture consists of two or more companies combining their resources to form a new company, as a separate entity from existing companies for the purpose of performing a contract. Once a contract is completed, the joint venture is dissolved a long with the new company that was formed to perform the contract.

BENEFITS OF TEAMING ARRANGEMENTS

- Building capacity
- Increases annual profits
- Work on large government procurements
- Increase working capital
- Expand/diversify products
- Network to develop strong business relationships

WHERE CAN YOU FIND TEAMING OPPORTUNITIES?

- Seek teaming opportunities through Small Business Programs also called supplier diversity programs. By contacting the supplier diversity offices, small businesses can network and develop relationships that can result in teaming opportunities and procurement awards?

MARKETING FOR SME'S

Marketing defined:

Marketing defined as a management process of identifying, anticipating and satisfying consumer needs and wants more effectively than a competitor.

What are Needs and Wants?

Unsatisfied human desires that motivate their actions and enhance their fulfillment when met.

Many business marketing departments pay close attention to the needs and wants of their target market since both drive consumer purchases. These can be further described as those needs that are based on biological necessities, and those wants that make life more pleasant and which largely depend on psychological factors.

Product Portfolio Matrix

A Perspective titled "The Product Portfolio "introduces the growth-share matrix. This framework categorizes products within a company's portfolio as stars, cash cows, dogs, or question marks according to growth rate, market share, and positive or negative cash flow. By using positive cash flows a company can capitalize on growth opportunities.

"The payoff for leadership [in market share] is very high indeed, if it is achieved early and maintained until growth slows," Bruce Henderson would tell clients. "Investment in market share during the growth phase can be very attractive, if you have the cash. Growth in market is compounded by growth in share. Increases in share increase the profit margin . . . The return on investment is enormous."24

E-MARKETING FOR SME'S

E-marketing is the use of information technology in the process of creating, communicating and delivering value to the customers and for managing customer relationships in ways that benefit the

Organization and its stakeholders. It's the application of information technology to traditional marketing practices.

E-business is the continuous optimization of a company's business activities through digital technology.

E-marketing environment offers opportunities to develop new products, new markets, new media and new channels.

Remember that E-commerce is the subset of E-business.

E-STRATEGY FOR SME'S

E-Business strategy is the deployment of enterprise resources to capitalize on technologies for reaching specific objectives that ultimately improve performance and create sustainable competitive advantage.

E-Marketing Strategy is the design of marketing strategy that capitalizes on organizations electronic or information technology capabilities to reach specific goals

THE IMPORTANCE OF E-MARKETING FOR SME'S

SME's needs E-business/E-commerce to survive in today's market

- Increases revenue to the organization
- Increase benefits to the products
- Decrease costs to the products

ETHICS AND
LEGAL ISSUES FOR SME'S

In reality Ethics and Law are related. Ethics really concerns the values and practices of the professionals and others who have expert knowledge of a specific field. Ethics is also a general endeavor that takes into account the concerns and values of society as a whole

Law is similar to ethics in that, it is an expression of values, while ethics may be directed to individual or groups.

E-MARKETERS needs data to guide decisions about creating and changing marketing mix elements

A Marketing Information System is the process by which marketers manage knowledge, using a system of assessing information needs, gathering information, analyzing it, and disseminating it to decision makers.

CONSUMER BEHAVIOR ONLINE

The internet has grown more quickly than any other medium. The basic marketing concept of exchange refers to the act of obtaining a desired object from someone by offering something in return.

Individual consumers bring their own characteristics and personal resources to the process as they seek specific outcomes from an exchange.

CONSUMER MARKET

The consumer market involves marketing goods and services to the end users

These are characterized by:

- Demographics
- Local markets
- Ethnic groups
- Interest communities
- Usage
- Benefit
- Behavior
- Attitude

CONSUMER BEHAVIOR

Consumer behavior is the study of individuals, groups, or organizations and the processes they use to select, secure, and dispose of products, services, experiences, or ideas to satisfy needs and the impacts that these processes have on the consumer and society.[1] It blends elements from psychology, sociology, social anthropology and economics. It attempts to understand the decision-making processes of buyers, both individually and in groups. It studies characteristics of individual consumers such as demographics and behavioral variables in an attempt to understand people's wants. It also tries to assess influences on the consumer from groups such as family, friends, reference groups, and society in general.

Customer behavior study is based on consumer buying behavior, with the customer playing the three distinct roles of user, payer and buyer. Research has shown that consumer behavior is difficult to predict, even for experts in the field.[2] Relationship marketing is an influential asset for customer behavior analysis as it has a keen interest in the re-discovery of the true meaning of marketing through the re-affirmation of the importance of the customer or buyer. A greater importance is also placed on consumer retention, customer relationship management, personalization, customization and one-to-one marketing. Social functions can be categorized into social choice and welfare functions.25

Marketing management must try to work out what goes on the in the mind of the customer—the "black box".

The Buyer's characteristics influence how he or she perceives the stimuli; the decision-making process determines what buying behavior is undertaken.

Characteristics that affect customer behavior

The first stage of understanding buyer behavior is to focus on the factors that determine he "buyer characteristics"

CONDITIONS WHERE CONSUMERS GAIN BARGAINING POWER

- If they can inexpensively switch
- If they are particularly important
- If sellers are struggling in the face of falling consumer demand
- If they are informed about the sellers' products, price, and costs
- If they have discretion in whether and when they purchase the product

MARKETING CULTURE

What is Market Culture?

Market Culture is a **relative term** to describe:

The overarching culture of a business relating to the attention it focuses on markets/customers

The skills used to create value for customers

The level of belief that the ultimate purpose of the business is to create superior customer value, profitably26

MARKET ANALYSIS, OUTLINE DIMENSIONS FOR SME'S

The goal of market analysis is to determine the attractiveness of a market and to understand its evolving opportunities and threats as they relate to the strengths and weaknesses of the firm.

The following is the outline dimensions of a market analysis:

Market size (current and future)
Market growth rate
Market profitability
Industry cost structure
Distribution channels
Market trends
Key success factors

MARKET SIZE

The size of the market can be evaluated based on present sales and potential sales if the use of the product were expanded. The following are information source for determining market size:

- Government data
- Trade associations
- Financial data from major players
- Customer surveys

MARKET GROWTH RATE

A simple means of forecasting the market growth rate is to extrapolate historical data into the future. This method may provide a first order estimate; it does not predict important turning points.

A better method is to study growth drivers such as:

- Demographic information
- Sales growth in complementary products

Such drivers save as leading indicators that are more accurate than simply extrapolating historical data.

Important inflection points in the market rate sometimes can be predicted by constructing a product diffusion curve. The shape of a curve can be estimated by studying the characteristics of the adoption rate of a similar product in the past.

The maturity and decline stages of a product life cycle will be reached.

Indicators of decline phase include price pressure caused by:

- Competition
- Decrease in brand loyalty
- Emergence of substitute products
- Market saturation
- Lack of growth drivers

MARKET PROFITABILITY

While different firms in a market will have different levels of profitability, the average profit potential for a market can be used as guideline for knowing how difficult it is to make money in the market.

The five factors influencing market profitability:

- Buyer power
- Supplier power
- Barriers to entry
- Threats of substitute products
- Rivalry among firms in the industry

MARKET TRENDS

- Changes in the market are important because they are source of:
- Opportunities and threats
- Price change sensitivity
- Demand for variety
- Level of emphasis on service and support

KEY SUCCESS FACTORS

- Access to essential unique resources
- Ability to achieve economies of scales
- Access to distribution channels
- Technological progress

It is important to consider that key success factors may change over time, especially as the product progresses through its life cycle.

INDUSTRY COST STRUCTURE

This is important for identifying key factors for success.

This is helpful for formulating strategies to develop a competitive advantage.

DISTRIBUTION CHANNELS

These are important in the market analysis:

Existing Distribution Channels—can be described by how direct they are to the customer

Trends and Emerging Channels—new channels can offer the opportunity to develop a competitive advantage

Channel Power Structure—for example, in the product having little brand equity, retailers have negotiating power over manufactures and can capture more margin

STRATEGY ANALYSIS

The evaluation of the TOWS Matrix for SME's yields a number of possible strategies that could be adopted. The following strategies are the top strategies based on potential profit contribution and company strengths and weaknesses:

- Perform research and development of new products and technologies to aid in the development new auto parts.
- Perform Market segmentation for easy customer service.
- Perform research and development of new products and technologies to aid in the prevention industrial espionage.
- Perform Product positioning strategy
- Customer retention should be number one objective.
- Customer satisfaction should be number one strategy.
- I would advice to use Marketing Intelligence System so often.

STRATEGY RECOMMENDATION

Prior to selecting alternative strategies for a company a thorough analysis of internal and external factors must be completed. This enables management to evaluate the company's internal position in relation to its external environment. By performing this analysis strategies can be selected that best match the company's abilities to the opportunities presented. Once a course of action for the company has been selected, an implementation strategy is required to ensure that all required aspects of the company's operations

- SME's must adopt a Marketing Culture.
- Market Opportunity analysis must be performed to answer questions like:-

1-Can we deliver the benefits better than a competitor?

2-Can we locate the target markets and reach them with cost-effective media and trade channels.

3-Will the financial rate of return meet our require threshold for investment.

4-Do we have access to the capabilities and resources needed to deliver the customer benefits?

5-Can we articulate the benefits convincingly to defined target markets?

EXTERNAL ENVIRONMENT

The SME's face an external environment that continues to evolve. These factors, which are beyond the control and influence of the company, have a great impact on the current and future earnings potential of each of the company's business units. Recognition of the potential external threats and opportunities presented to the company and the associated response by management is a key factor in the company's future success.

FUTURE FACTORS

The external factor that could have the greatest impact on future profit potentials is the increase in deficit spending by the United States government. As the budget deficit continues to grow, there will be increased pressure from Congress and their constituents to decrease spending. This could lead to budget cuts that would affect all five of the company's business units.

President Obama's announcement of a renewed focus and effort on auto industry and future bailout of auto makers by providing stimulus packages opens many future opportunities for Parts Authority. The President proposed increases in bailout's budget this year and the years to come to fund the research and development of the technologies and auto makers are required to create more jobs the country men and women to combat the economy that will lead to more consumer spending.

The auto industry continues to struggle following the recession in 2009. However, as public confidence in auto industry increases, the number of buyers that chose to buy vehicle is steadily increasing. The number of daily auto parts buyer's increases near the levels prior to the recession. The increases in the buying power have spurred several small, low cost startup companies. As the number of small business increases parts Authority will continue to supply parts to keep up with the increase market demand that is quickly becoming saturated.

The future threat of industrial espionage cannot be overlooked. Because 78 percent of Parts Authority business is with the private sector, the company is a prime target for espionage from foreign rival businesses. The company continues to mitigate the chances of confidential information for being compromised by continually updating and employing the most state of the art intrusion marketers. However, there is a chance that the most state of the art marketer will not be available to combat all future espionage attempts.

The likelihood of a future recession event occurring on United States soil is a very real possibility. While an event such as this would continue to offer opportunities to Parts Authority, it would also threaten other potential profit generating initiatives. Parts Authority is already spending enormous amounts of money on the promotion activities. Another recession would likely lead to increases in Parts Authority spending in these areas, but not enough to offset loses if their budget decreases in other profit generating areas not related to auto industry. Government Funding for auto industry would likely be cut to make up for the increased spending on small businesses.

EXTERNAL FACTOR
EVALUATION MATRIX (TABLE 1)

Key External Factors	Weight	Rating	Weighted Score	% of Weight Score
Opportunities				
1. Recession	.10	4	.40	15
2. Stimulus Package	.20	4	.80	30
3. Future conflicts	.05	3	.15	6
4. Auto industry	.10	3	.30	11
5. Public confidence in auto industry	.05	2	.10	4
Subtotal	.50		1.75	66
Threats				
1. U.S. high tech trade regulations	.10	2	.20	7
2. EU trade regulations	.10	2	.20	7

3. Budget deficit	.15	1	.15	6
4. Industrial espionage	.10	3	.30	11
5. Terrorist event	.05	2	.10	4
Subtotal	.50		.95	35
Total	**1.00**		**2.70**	100

Weight: *0-1 representing percentage of potential contribution to profit growth.*

Rating: *1-4 representing the company's ability to respond to given factor with one being the worst prepared and four being the best.*

FUTURE DIRECTION

Based on current economic situation and the likelihood of a prolonged recession, Parts Authority is positioned well to take advantage of the opportunities presented. The weighted score of 2.70 in the external factor evaluation matrix indicates that the company has an above average ability to address opportunities and threats that are beyond its control or influence. However, the Parts Authority is not positioned well to mitigate the potential threat of decreases in government spending or tightening trade restrictions by the United States government and the European Union. Parts Authority could better position itself by using its advanced technology to develop high quality consumer products that would not be scrutinized by government export restrictions or be tied to government spending.

COMPETITION

Parts Authority is one of leading auto supplier that provide auto parts and services to the private sector. Prior to matching alternative long-term strategies to the company's internal strength and weaknesses to the external environments threats and opportunities, an assessment of its position as related to its closest competitors must be done. After the company's position has been evaluated, an appropriate decision can be made that will determine the company's long-term business strategy.

PRESENT COMPETITION

Based on auto parts supply industry report by Robert Friedman, Parts Authority's two primary competitors are the Advance Auto and Pep boys companies. Based on 2008 revenues, Advanced Auto accounted for 87.8 percent of Parts Authority, 40.8 percent of Advanced Auto and 91.2 percent of Pep boy's total revenue.

PRODUCT MARKET AND DISTRIBUTION

Both the Advanced Auto and Pep boys companies have commercial as well as government related business segments that compete with Parts Authority's. The Advanced Auto Company's major focus is on the private industry and is currently in direct competition with Pep Boys to be the largest provider of auto parts. However, the Advanced Auto Company's market segment competes directly with Parts Authority in the private sectors, government market. Pep Boys provides commercial sales of electronic systems and services, but a majority of its revenues comes from its auto parts sales.

COMPETITIVE ADVANTAGES

The competitive advantage that Parts Authority holds over the Advanced Auto Company and Pep boys Company primarily is its focus on serving the auto industry and other United States government agencies. This focus has enabled the company to best utilize its research and development to generate new products and innovations that serve the private sectors. Additionally, Parts Authority's lengthy history of providing products and services primarily to these government sectors has enabled it to establish long-standing contacts, anticipate future needs and to influence future contracts with the government. Finally, Parts Authority's financial position has enabled it to purchase Southern Auto Parts that will help it compete with other emerging auto parts suppliers.

COMPETITIVE DISADVANTAGES

The disadvantage Parts Authority faces comes from its limited product line. The systems that they develop have limited application in the commercial market or cannot be sold commercially or exported due to government regulations. Additionally, Parts Authority is an expert in distribution and integration, but the majority of the commercial off the shelf parts that they utilize in are built by one of their prime competitors, Mawdi. Finally, because of Parts Authority's focus on the government market the profitability is tied to world crisis, were their other competitors have products that have commercial applicability as well.

COMPETITIVE PROFILE MATRIX

The competitive profile matrix, (table 2) identifies the factors critical to the success of a company or business segment operating in the Auto parts industry. As shown in table 2, Parts Authority dominates the private sector as compared to its two closest competitors. Parts Authority focuses almost all its resources on products and services related to the auto industry. This accounts for its dominance in auto related R&D, and market share. The Advanced auto Company lags in this area, because a majority of its product line and R&D are tied up competing with retail stores in the commercial parts industry. The size and limited resources of the Pep Boys Company limits the size of the product line and services they can provide. Additionally, their limited financial ability has impacted their market share and the exposure they would need to build greater customer loyalty.

COMPETITIVE PROFILE MATRIX (TABLE 2)

Critical Success Factors	Weight	Parts Authority		Advanced Auto		Pep boy's	
		Rating	Score	Rating	Score	Rating	Score
Product line	.15	3	.45	2	.30	2	.30
R&D	.25	4	1.00	3	.75	3	.75
Financial strength	.20	3	.60	4	.80	2	.40
Customer loyalty	.10	3	.30	2	.20	2	.20
Product quality	.15	3	.45	3	.45	3	.45
Market Share	.15	4	.60	3	.45	1	.15
Total	1.00		3.40		2.95		2.25

Rating values: *1=major weakness, 2=minor weakness, 3=minor strength, 4=major strength*

FUTURE COMPETITION

Advanced Auto and Pep Boy's are going to continue to be Parts Authority greatest competitors. In the future, Advanced Auto may adjust its long-term strategies to take advantage of the increases in funding to the Auto industry. If Advanced Auto loses market share in the commercial Auto parts industry to Pep Boys, an increased focus on auto related products and services if even more likely to occur to make up for lost revenues. The increases in spending on auto will also aid Pep Boy's growth and expansion in the auto parts industry as well. Since over 90 percent of Pep Boy's revenues are generated from products and services in this industry, they are likely to experience increased profits from future contracts with the government. Even though Pep Boys scored significantly lower on the competitive profile matrix, they present a great threat to Parts Authority, because they focus almost all their resources on the Auto parts industry such as Parts Authority.

CONCLUSION

Prior to performing a strategic analysis to determine possible long-term strategies a through assessment of the external environment and the company's competitors must be performed. Because of the current world environment, Parts Authority is poised to take advantage of the opportunities presented. However, attention needs to be given to the narrow scope of Parts Authority's business operations, so it can take advantage of other markets. Finally, Parts Authority currently leads the competition as the premier provider of products and services to the total market. But the increase in government spending is going to spur new competition and make current competitors stronger and more difficult to keep at bay.

REFERENCES

Book, Elizabeth G. *Info-Tech Industry Targets Diverse Threats*. August 2002. Online. Acessed: 18 June 2004. *http://www.nationaldefensemagazine. org/*

STRATEGY IMPLEMENTATION

The SME's must meet key milestones to enable it to meet the goal of a 20 percent increase in market share over the next five years. The objective presented and the timeline provided apply to all five of Parts Authority business units. Additionally, a pro forma statement of operations is provided to illustrate the changes in revenues attributed to increased market share over the next five years. The pro forma statement of operations is based on a linear increase in market share over the time frame. However, increases in market share may be more concentrated in some years than others.

TIMELINE

The following timeline is representative of the objectives required of all five business units to meet the goal of increased market share. The time line for implementing the changes in long-term strategies is based on the date of final determination of the specific strategy. The timeline indicates the deadline for completing the assigned objectives. Many of the objectives run concurrently. market penetration and/or product development are consistent with a hold and maintain strategy for a company.

Based on the above criteria for strategy selection the most potentially profitable strategy that best addresses the external environment and the company's internal capabilities is increasing research and development to improve or develop new products and services to meet current and future auto needs of the vehicle manufactured in the United States government.

Increase market share of SME's by twenty percent over the next five years, by increasing research, development and testing to develop new or improved products that will fulfill a key consumer needs.

I would emphasize on using Marketing Intelligence System that supply happening data.

Also market analysis must be performed periodically

SITUATION ANALYSIS FOR SME'S

In order to satisfy customer needs, SME's must understand its external and internal situation, including:

- Customer
- Market environment
- Firms own capabilities

The frame work for performing a situation analysis which covers:

- Internal
- Micro-environment
- Macro-environment

is the **5 C Analysis;** Company, Collaborator, Customers, Competitors and Climate (or context).

The 5 C Analysis is outlined below:

Company:

- Product line
- Image in the market
- Technology and experience
- Culture
- Goals

Collaborators

- Distributors
- Suppliers
- Alliances
    Customers:
- Market size and growth
- Market segments
- Customer benefits, tangible and intangible
- Motivation behind purchase; value drivers, benefits vs. costs
- Decision maker or decision—making unit
- Retail channel-where does the customer purchase the product
- Customer information source-where does the customer obtain information about the product
- Buying process e.g. impulse or careful comparison
- Frequency of purchase—seasonal factors
- Quality purchase at a time
- Trends—how customer needs and preferences change over time

Competitors:

- Actual or potential
- Direct or indirect
- Products
- Positioning
- Market shares
- Strengths and weaknesses of competitors

Climate (or context)

Often referred to as a PEST Analysis, four external "climate" or macro-environmental factors are:

- **P**olitical & regulatory environment—government policies and regulation that affect the market
- **E**conomic environment—business cycle, inflation, interest rate, and other macroeconomic issues
- **S**ocial/cultural environment—society's trends and fashion

- Technological environment-new knowledge that makes possible new ways of satisfying needs; the impact of technology on the demand for existing products.

INFORMATION SOURCES:

Customer and competitor information specifically oriented toward marketing decisions can be found in market research reports, which provide a market analysis for a particular industry. For foreign markets, country reports can be used as a general information source for the macro-environment. By combining regional and market analysis with knowledge of the firm's own capabilities and partnerships, the firm can identify and select the more favorable opportunities to provide value to the customer.

BUSINESS PROJECT MANAGEMENT FOR SME'S

WHAT IS EARNED VALUE?

Technique that relates resource planning to

- Schedules
- Technical costs
- Schedule requirements

All work is planned, budgeted, and scheduled in time-phased "planned value" increments constituting a cost and schedule measurement baseline.

Major objectives are:

- Encourage the use of effective internal cost and schedule management control systems;
- Permit the customer to be able to rely on timely data produced by those systems for determining product-oriented contract status

END VALUE DEFINED

- It compares the planned amount of work with what has actually been completed, to determine if costs, schedule, and work accomplished are progressing as planned
- Work is "Earned" or credited as it is completed.

WHY EARNED VALUE

- Different measures of progress for different types of tasks
- Need to "roll up" progress of many tasks into an overall project status
- Need for a uniform unit of measure (dollars or work-hours)
- Allows measurement of a project's progress
- increases accuracy of forecast completion date and final cost
- provides insight into schedule and budgets variances
- Provides consistent, numerical indicators with which you can evaluate and compare projects

MANAGEMENT SUPPORT FOR EARNED VALUE

-   Provide an "Early Warning" signal for prompt corrective action.

Bad news does not age well

Still time to recover

Timely request for additional funds

TERMS DEFINED

PV-PLANNED VALUE (BCWS)

Budgeted costs of the total amount of work scheduled to be performed by the milestone date

AC-ACTUAL COSTS (ACWP)

Cost incurred to accomplish the work that been done to date

EV-EARNED VALUE (BCWP)

The planned (not actual) cost to complete the work that has been done

DERIVED METRIX

SV-SCHEDULE VARIANCE (EV-PV)

- A comparison of amount of work performed during a given period of time to what was scheduled to be performed.
- A negative variance means the project is behind schedule.

CV-COST VARIANCE (EV-AC)

- A comparison of the budgeted cost of work performed with actual cost
- A negative variance means the project is over budget.

SV-SCHEDULE VARIANCE (BCWP-ACWP)

- A comparison of amount of work performed during a given period of time to what was scheduled to be performed
- A negative variance means the project is behind schedule

CV-COST VARIANCE (BCWP-ACWP)

- A comparison of the budgeted cost of work performed with actual cost
- A negative variance means the project is over budget

WORK BREAKDOWN STRUCTURE

A work breakdown structure from a previous project can often be used as a template for a new project.

Although each project is unique, WBS's can often be "reused" since most projects will resemble another project to some extent.

- For example, most projects will have the same or similar project life cycles and will thus have the same or similar deliverables required from each phase.

DECOMPOSITION OF A PROJECT

Decomposition involves subdividing the major project deliverables into smaller, more manageable components until the deliverables are defined in sufficient details to support future project activities (planning, executing, controlling and closing).

WORK PACKAGES DEFINED

- Each item in the WBS is generally assigned a unique Identifier; these identifiers are often known collectively as the code of accounts
- The items at the lowest level of the WBS are often referred to as work packages. These work packages are further decomposed into activities (the activities necessary to produce the deliverables), though this is correctly now part of activity definition and is part of the project time management.

ACTIVITY DEFINITION

Activity definition involves identifying and documenting the specific activities that must be performed in order to produce the deliverables and sub deliverables identified in the work breakdown structure.

Implicit is this process is the need to define the activities such that the project objectives will be met

Activity definition starts with the work breakdown structure and scope statement

OUTPUTS FROM
ACTIVITY DEFINITION

Activity list. The activity list must include all activities which will be performed on the project. It should be organized as an extension to the WBS to help ensure that it is complete and that it does not include any activities which are not required as part of the project scope. As with the WBS, the activity list should include the descriptions of each activity to ensure that the project team members will understand how the work will be done.

Work breakdown structure updates. In using the WBS to identify which activities are needed, the project team may identify missing deliverable description or may determine that the deliverable descriptions need to be clarified or corrected. Any such updates must be reflected in the WBS and related documentation such as schedule basis of estimates (BOE). These updates are often called refinements and are most likely when the project involves new or unproven technology.

OUTPUT FROM ACTIVITY SEQUENCING

Project network diagram. A project network diagram is schematic display of the project activities and the logical relationships (dependencies) among them. A project network diagram may be produced manually or on a computer. The diagram should be accompanied by a summary narrative that describes the basic the basic sequences should be fully described.

PROJECT MANAGEMENT: PERT/CPM

o   Assist project management in planning and controlling of resources e.g., people, money, equipment, etc. to achieve time, cost and other goals of non-repetitive projects.
- Use of Gantt Chart—bar chart showing time and sequence of activities.
- PERT: Program Evaluation and Review Techniques. Developed by Navy for the Polaris Missile Project (1957-58)
  - Activity-on-Arrow (AOA) network representation
- CPM: Critical Path Method. Developed by Du Pont (1957)
  - Activity-on-Node (AON) network representation
  - Deterministic time estimates

o   Distinction between PERT and CPM is now blurred, and the terms are now used interchangeably.

PERT/CPM: ADVANTAGES

o   Project completion time estimate—deterministic or probabilistic
o   Effect of delay in one activity on the completion of the project.
o   Identifying activities that are critical for project's success (e.g., completion on time). Critical activities deserve close management attention and control.
o   Effective resource allocation (e.g., spending more, or moving people, to expedite critical activities)
o   Good tool for communication—initial plan and status update.
o   PERT charts do not show task durations graphically and may be difficult to read.
o   PERT charts are difficult to analyze without computer support.
o   PERT charts are difficult to use for project tracking without computer support
o   **Activity**: Operation that requires resource/s for completion.
o   **Event**: A point in time when either started or completed.
o   **Predecessor Activity**: An activity that must be completed before a given activity may be started.
o   **Path**: Sequence of activities that connect "project start" event to "project end" event.
o   **Critical Path**: Path having the longest duration.
o   **Slack time** for an activity: Duration by which an activity may be delayed without delaying the overall completion of the project.

COMPARE AND ITERATE ESTIMATE

o   There will always be differences in estimates. By understanding different results, you can more accurately estimate the costs in your situation. There may be other factors at work in the estimate that will affect the results.

- **Optimist / Pessimist phenomenon**

Similar components with different costs may b due to the mindset of the person estimating

Estimate = (1*a) + (4*m) + (1*b)

$$6$$

a = *most optimistic time*

b = *most pessimistic time*

m = *most likely time*

SUCCESS STRATEGIES FOR TAKING YOUR BUSINESS TO THE NEXT LEVEL

KEY TOPICS

- Business Etiquettes 101
- Standing Out Among Your Peers
- Contracting with the private sector
- What to do when you don't win the contract
- Proven Success Strategies
- Getting Your Foot in the door, in the federal sector
- Positioning your business to succeed.

BUSINESS ETIQUETTES 101

- Respect "other folks" time
- Respond to enquiries promptly
- Negotiate milestone deadlines that you can meet.
- Ask "is it the good time for us to talk? When you call a client, even if the call was scheduled in advance.
- Don't discuss race, religion or politics with your potential clients or in the work place
- Meetings Etiquette
- - Arrive on time
- - Give a firm handshake
- - Bring appropriate materials to the meeting and bring enough copies
- - Dress for the occasion
- - Always exhibit a professional demeanor.

STANDING OUT
AMONG YOUR PEERS

- Website should consist of your company name as the domain as (e.g. *www.diamondalefoundation.org*)
- Email address should include company name
- Business cards, brochures, capability statement should represent your company, clearly state your products/services, include all pertinent information(e.g. name, phone numbers, email address, website.
- Offering best customer service should be your goal

CONTRACTING WITH THE PRIVATE SECTOR

- Number of years in business, net worth, past experience, ability to respond timely, annual revenue, the number of employees, ability to follow instructions, preparation and submission of bids, offers etc.

WHAT TO DO WHEN YOU DON'T WIN A CONTRACT

- Ask for debriefing
- Consider reaching out to successful contractors.
- Know the difference between goals and entitlement.
- Price it right.

GETTING YOUR FOOT
IN THE DOOR

- Prime contracting—Your company holds the contract
- Subcontracting—a larger company holds the contract and your company gets to work on a portion of it.
- Joint venture, Partnership or Team with a competitor.
- Know where to look for contracting opportunities
- Identify and connect with the appropriate staff
- Hire the right people to represent your company
- Identify a mentor or someone who cares about your success.

POSITIONING YOUR BUSINESS TO SUCCEED

- Internet presence(website)
- Develop business plan
- Obtain business Insurance
- Financially sound
- Market your skills
- Know your customers/clients
- Look for partners
- Get certifications
- Diversify your clients
- Do your home work (Industry, Competitors, Market Research)

NETWORKING OPPORTUNITIES

- Business Networking sessions
- Briefing on major procurements and development projects
- Webinars
- Workshops
- Conferences
- Pre-proposal/pre-bid

www.ingramcontent.com/pod-product-compliance
Lightning Source LLC
Chambersburg PA
CBHW030009190526

45157CB00014B/1694